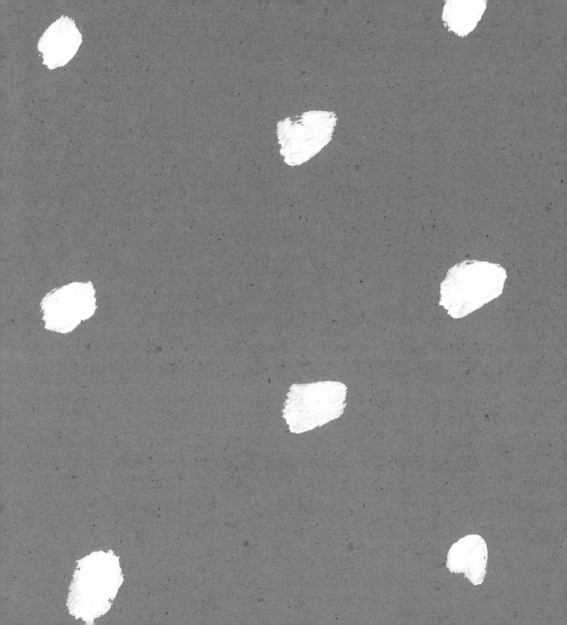

I love you more than . . .

pictures and verse
by
Sandra Magsamen

gift

stewart tabori & chang

This is
what I
know is
true...

every
word is
all
for you.

My heart
has spoken
loud and
clear

and
written this
poem for
you, my dear.

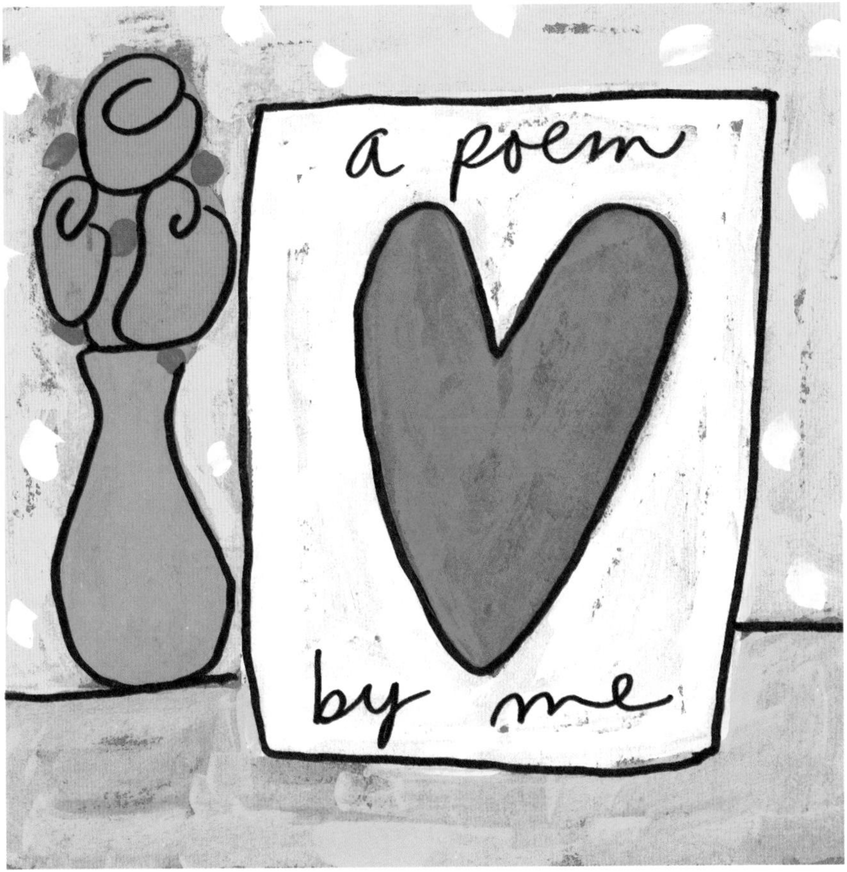
a poem
by me

I

love you

more than...

all the
leaves on
all the
trees

and all
the fish
in all
the seas.

All the stars that twinkle at night

and all the smiles that are shiny and bright.

All the
red roses
that climb
up the wall

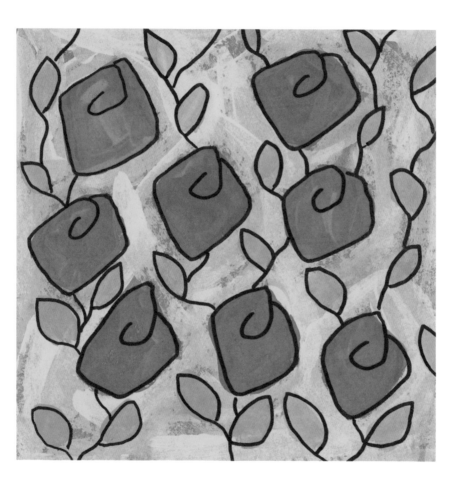

and each
rain drop
that will
ever fall.

All the kisses that have ever been given

and all the
"I'm sorry's"
and the
"you are
forgiven's".

I love you more than every bird that's colored blue

I love you,
because
you are you.

Pictures and verse by Sandra Magsamen
© 2001 Hanny Girl Productions, Inc.

Published in 2001 by
Stewart, Tabori & Chang
A division of Harry N. Abrams, Inc.
115 West 18th Street
New York, NY 10011

Distributed in Canada by
General Publishing Company Ltd.
30 Lesmill Road
Don Mills, Ontario, Canada M3B2J6

ISBN: 1-58479-068-7

Printed in Hong Kong

10 9 8 7 6 5 4 3 2 1